Shoals of Starlings

ANDREW MARTIN

WATERHARE
PRESS

SHOALS OF STARLINGS
A WATERHARE PRESS BOOK
ISBN: 978-1-9993112-4-7

First Edition: 1st June 2020
Edited by Richard Hamer

Waterhare Press is based in Plymouth, UK
waterharepress@publicist.com

About the author

Andrew Martin currently lives and works in Plymouth. He studied wildlife illustration in Carmarthen, South Wales, which has imbued his writing and artwork with elemental and natural world imagery. Writing poetry for him shares the same creative processes he uses in the generation of his digital pictures. Fractured fractals, shattered symmetries, images bleed and repeat, shift and change into each other, like variations on a theme in music. This is his first collection of poems and pictures.

Foreword by Steve Spence

Andrew Martin's debut collection is a rare mix of poetry and visual art in the sense that both mediums complement each other and are generated through similar thought processes. Andrew's poetry is a fine example of the modern lyric, writing about nature which fuses observation with psychological input, the author as an imaginative interpreter of the natural world, an interpretation which is both minimalist and full of musicality, fractured and filled with beautiful phrases and arresting imagery. There is also vulnerability here, and I'm reminded of John Clare's writing both in terms of the subject matter and the approach. The images themselves are close to abstraction yet hint at representation in the capture of movement, of swarming and of life, variations on a theme. This collection manages to combine the modern with the traditional in an exceptionally accomplished manner, a fine first book from a writer/artist I feel we are going to hear more about.

With special thanks to
Steve Spence
Thom Boulton
Richard Hamer
Caroline Chambers
and my parents
for their help, encouragement, and support.

Contents

Inside the Piano

Beneath the still puddle
of its midnight lid
frosted in dust
starlings line its strings
simmering the dark
charging the silence

Song Thrush

Raw umber
streaks your breast
song paint
soil has anointed you

brimful with half-lights
wake from dreams
of wind-blown-wheat

your small wingspan
wider than two open windows
daylight flare

fire throat
slit by flames
spill of grain

place a scalpel
against the sky's
swollen belly

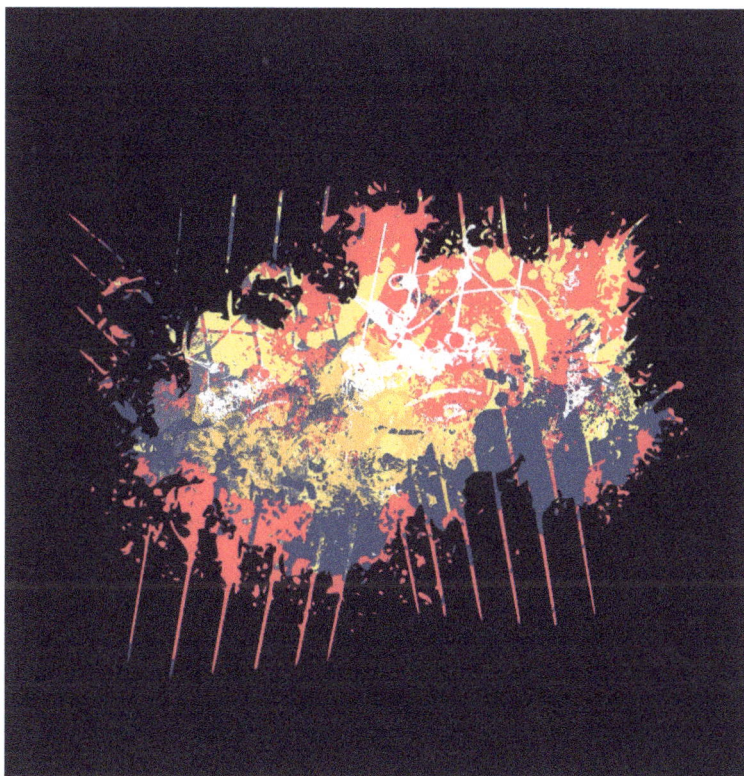

showers of sequins
mirrorball crumbled

dance floor sticky
congealed sunlight
spilt moonlight

trembling tinder box
your songs burn a second time
smoulder at night

smoke wraps me
is there a way
to will the heart to stop?

silence settles
in the charred church

songs re-smelted
in the crucible of the font

soil dips its fingers

Wrens

Soot sprites of the hedgerows
lacing sunlight between darknesses
stitching shadows together

Wren

Escaped hummingbird
spent its life down the pits
keeps to the shadows now

sipping from primroses
and the splashes of light
along the edge of fields

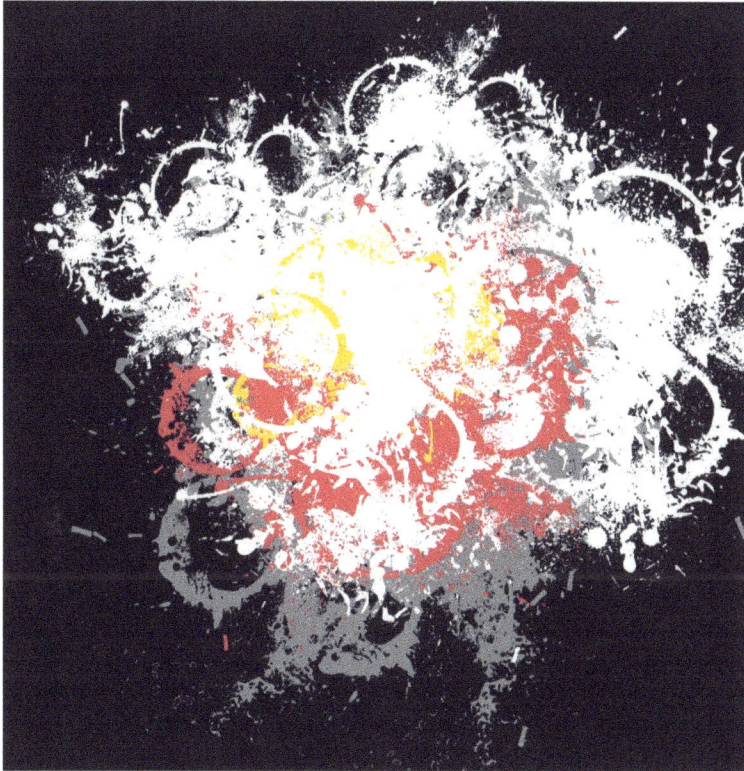

Hummingbirds

With needle-thin tongues
the ice blue of their feathers
cools them enough
to sip at the sun

A Static of Starlings

Blizzard
fresh from ballet school
sheet of perfect symmetry
turns dark upon breaking
instantly trying
to smelt back together again

are we not all trying to synchronise?
to fly as close together as possible
without touching
to make the darkness shimmer
to tune into the clearness
of a silence

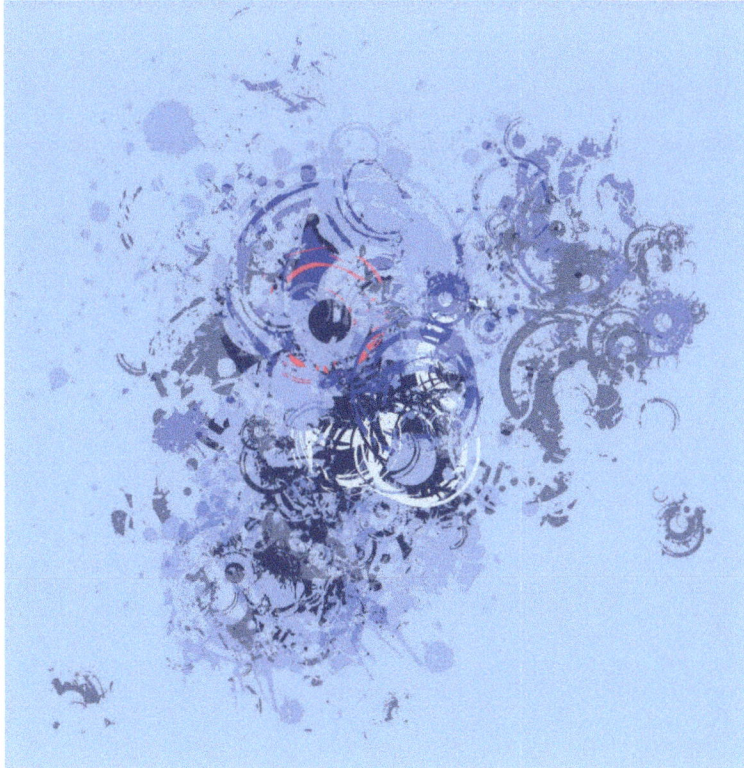

Coal Tit

Crumbling from the core
thumbprint from a ghost
a moth in sunlight

Blue Tit

You mutant bumblebee
powered in blue
dusted in the pollen
from a clear sky

Swifts

Born like switchblades
flicked open
locked open

sky takes root in their brains
cracks open their
small-as-seeds-hearts

bones full with fever
scribbling infinities
above the fields

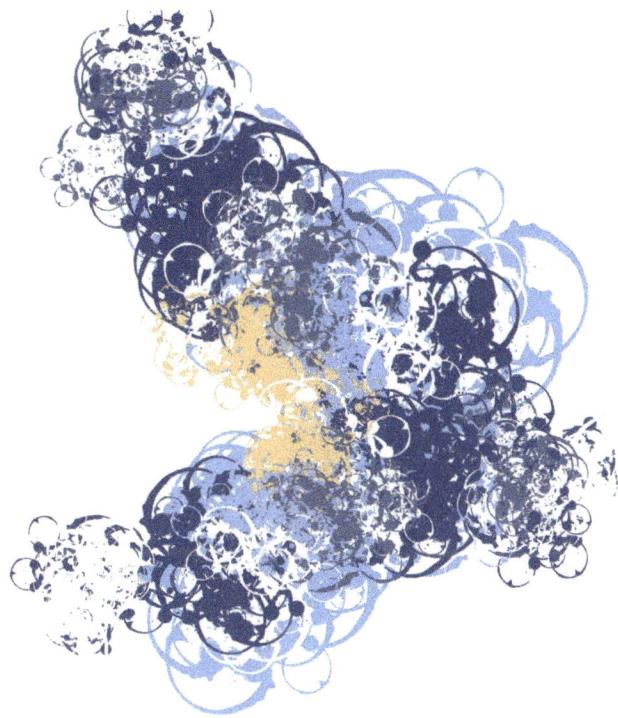

Swallows

1.

Blue blazes
in the charred rafters
of their brains

forked tails quivering
tuning forks
struck on the sky

2.

Seamstresses
scissoring the sky

swallow their reflections
and the blood on their bellies

House Martins

Ice skating in the wind
cutting and closing
the wound

their jet trails
dissolvable stitches
fading back into sky

their graceful surgery
leaves no trace
scars like smoke

memory of home
the whisper of grey
tugged into air

Crow

Born from snow
heart riddled with smoke
haunted by dreams of swans

Swan

Diamond
crushed from coal

swan
crushed from crows

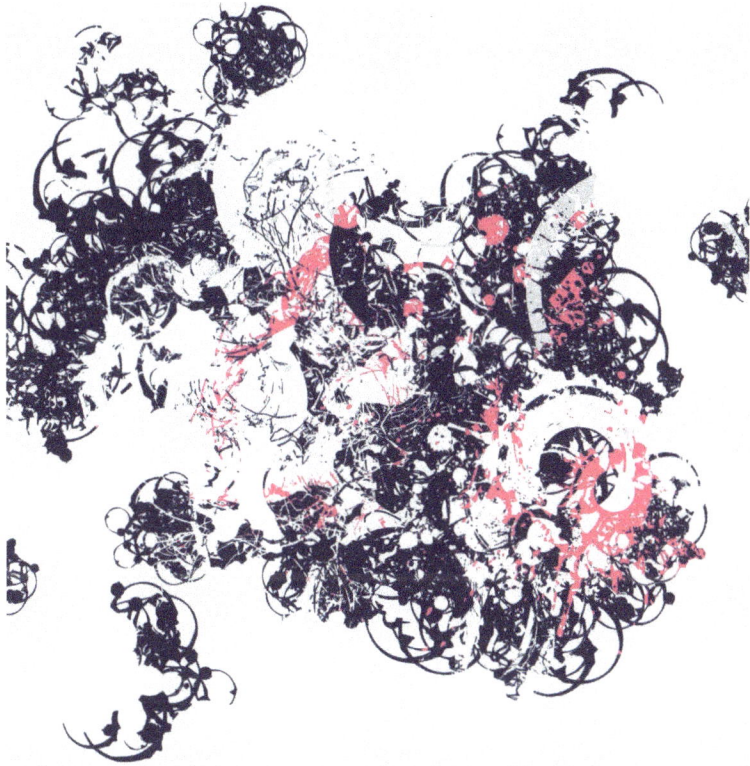

Magpie

Swan stalled
turning back to crow
slag of silver brain
still cooling
still haunted
by the cupped palms
of the crucible

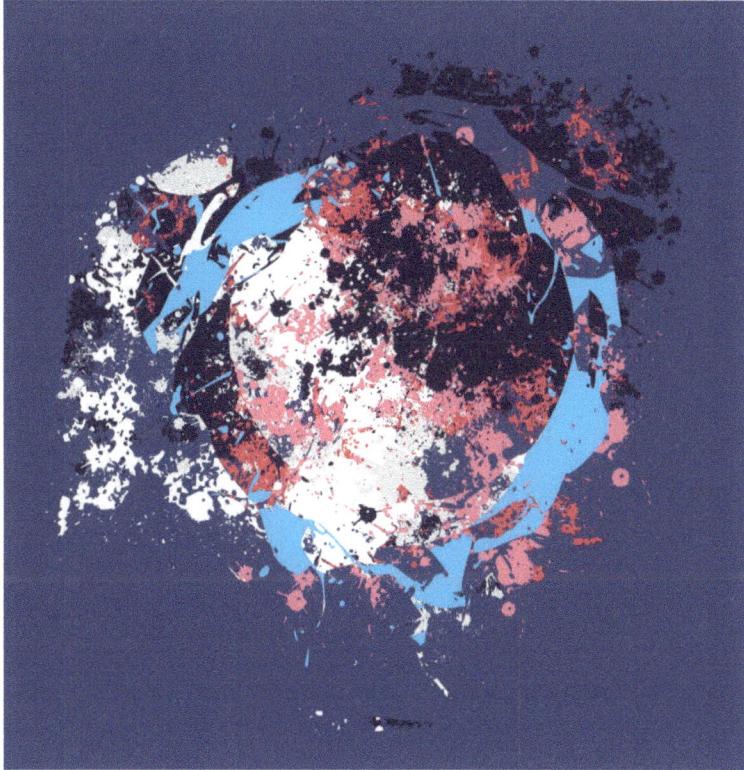

Jackdaws

Starlings on steroids
swallowed all their stars

storm bathing
lightning cleansing their souls

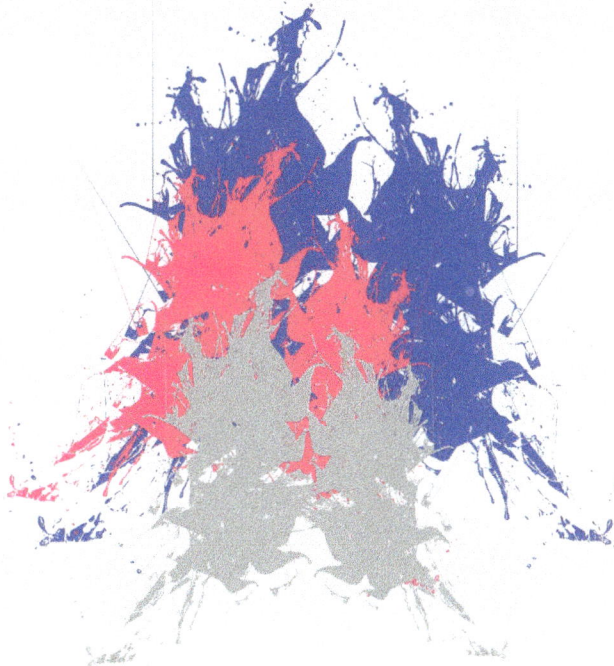

Birthday Gifts

For Caroline

Gave you darknesses
for your birthday
silhouettes and shadows
places where light
wishes it could go
the blinding black
of a crow's heart
thick with stars

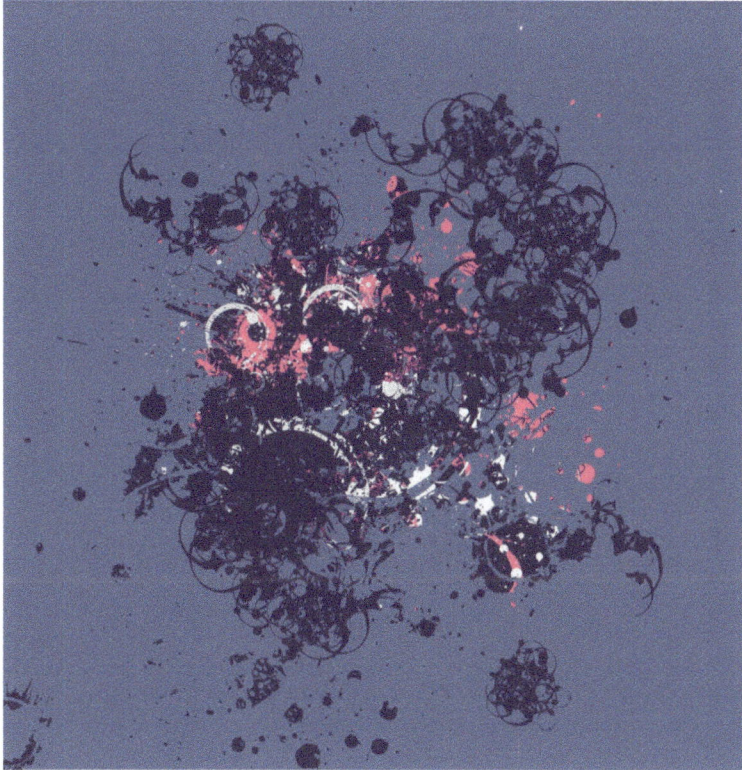

Raven

Black beaten into you
by the blacksmith
everything tastes of anvil
hacking up snake skins

the bark of the sun
echoes through the grass
pure chimney
solder trickling into sky

how the stars peek
over the rim of the well
come to see the caged
curled around embers

the wind worries
lifts and examines
the stained bandages
of your song

the lining torn
from your throat

A Silence of Swans

White-hot
raised their core temperature
the river will not swallow them

Peregrine

Desire to dive
woven into its wings

spearheads
sequin its chest

constriction of pupils
channelling its sight

before channelling the air
around its collapsed sails

blade of slate
plunged into snow

heart implodes
almost disappears

a second before
it explodes

Pigeons

1.

Softened slate
absorbed the rain
from a firework
blush in a storm

2.

The bang ping-ponged
until exhausted
comes to rest in the corner
cooing a song
into the bowl of its hands

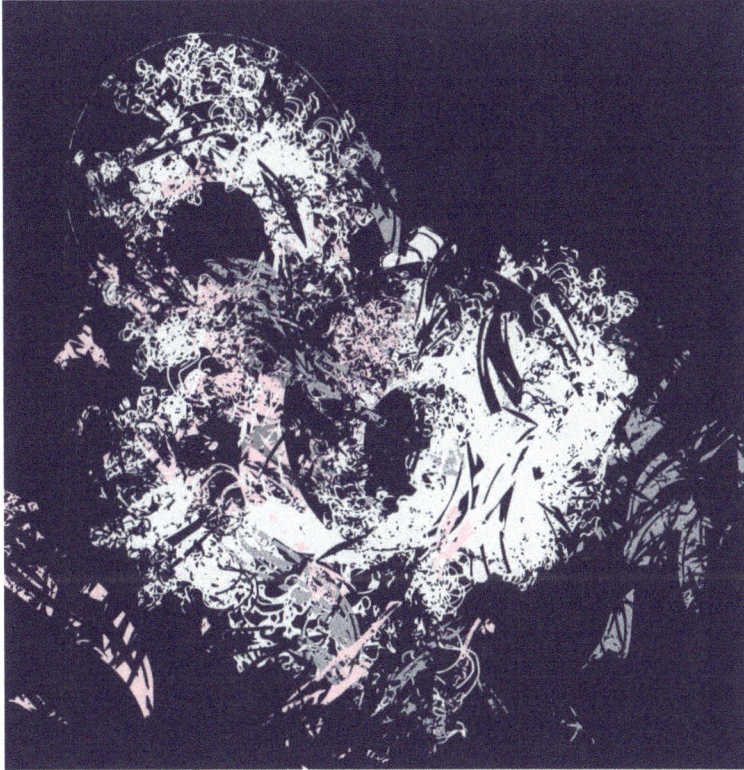

3.

Stained glass light
sun staring down
through the rose window
of a rainbow umbrella
staining the seal skin
of the pavement

4.

Coals cradle you to sleep
feathers falling
from the charred heavens

5.

Charcoal surprises
magic in the marks it makes
blaze bright as crayons
wielded by children
scribbling their spells

Kingfishers

1.

Shock of blue
fragment of dragon

breast scaled
in beaten fire
water cannot cool

full of bad wiring
heart always shorting

dives to slow
the neon lightning
that ribbons from him

2.

Scaled in the scales
of slain dragonflies
knight of the river
that has already started
to rust you
that will sing you
down to a spark

Buzzard

Following the scent
of the thermals
spiralling up and down
the spiral staircases
tearing the hearts
out of roadkill
giving them a sky burial

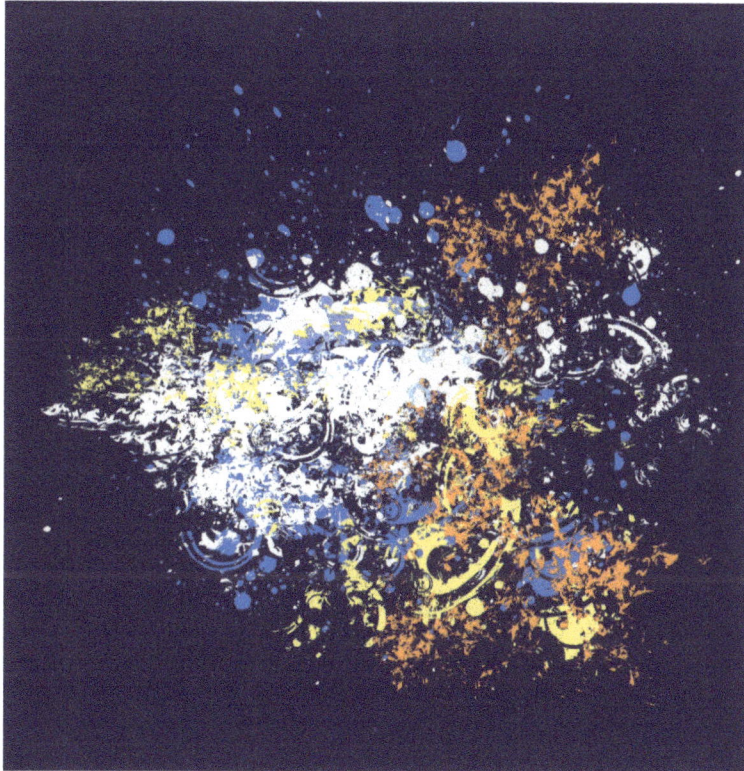

Gulls

Instantly pales
snapped from the sea
hunger aches
in their stomachs

cry for the darkness
lost at birth
cries like long slivers
of broken glass
pulled from the skin

the drunk sword swallower
laughing as he extracts the blade
a snot of clot
screams across
the reflected sky

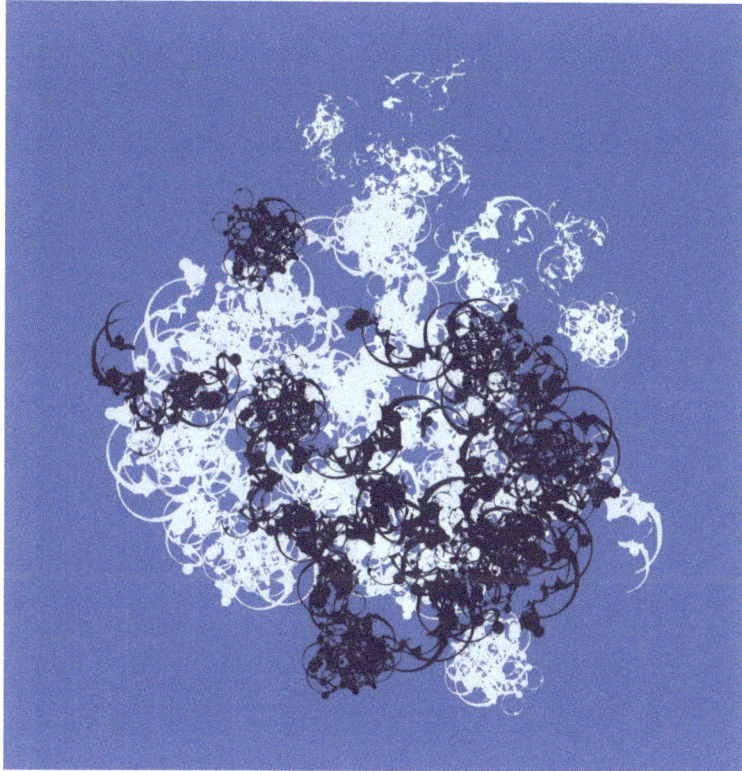

Gull

Returning home
we sigh like the opened valves of our airbeds

memories beginning to peak
handkerchiefs from our sleeves

sand like crumbs of gold
caught in the valleys of our books

wash the sea from our hair
hear its hush as we pull back the sheets

we wake with a start
as if the dark had cried

the white of a gull

Thief

A seagull stole your shoe
I can understand why
it wanted something
that had held a part of you

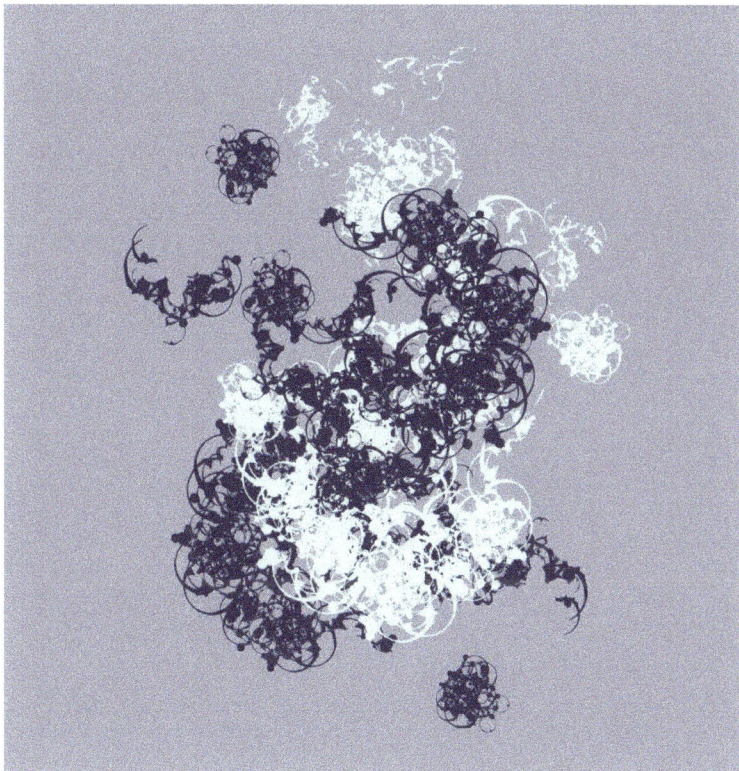

Blackbirds

1.

Reveals the engine room
at the bottom of its throat
stoked with song

2.

Body singed
by the flame
of its beak
psalms of smoke
tangled inside
a little life
long with song

3.

Born in blackness
explodes
brought into sky
spraying song like blood

Red-Winged Blackbird

1.

Am I the bottom of your blades
farthest from the sky
glowing the vermilion
of a freshly peeled scalp
am I buried in the coals
of your still smouldering
shuddering heart

am I the sunlight
dusting the midnight
of your belly?
the whisper of white
the trickle of smoke
in the sleep of your womb?

am I the fire
stuck in your throat
the burning of grass
trying to sing
into the currents
of a frayed wind?

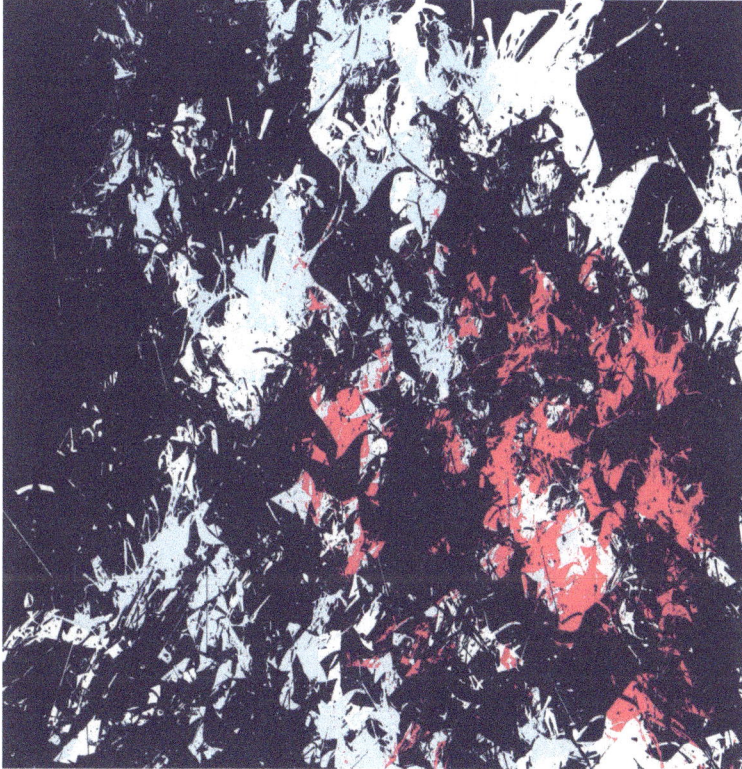

2.

Feathers spark
brushing against the dark
remnants of a spell
fading
in the muted sunlight

everyone stops breathing
in the same second
white words
dropped like teeth
into snow

shooting dead stars
fall from the night
charred sheriff badges
burrowing back
into white

Jay

Sky has sheathed its blue
blades into your wings

not deep enough
to hold them up to the hilt

Stellar Jay

Feathers carbonised and jewelled
the colour of expired dilithium crystals
you've flown through the heart of stars

now you rest
listening to the dust settle
on the skin of a river

Tawny Owl

Old nebula
brain blooming
with clouds of rust

call to your clone

together
from the smelted blacks
of your eyes
with silent hammers

beat out
another autumn sun

A Haunting

Wingtips dipped in dawn
ghosts with bodies
haunting and haunted
powdered in fire
stained by sun
dissolving from the inside
gold smoke curls against
the roof of their skulls
before rocking down
slow in the still air
slow like snow
snow like shrapnel
embedding itself
in our dark fields
the paleness of scars
sealing them in
the whiteness
of their silent blades
rusting deep inside us

Barn Owl

Moon a mirror
cut from
swathes of spirits
sown together
with muted gold
and silver thread
your face funnels moonlight
into the midnight wells
of your eyes
their polished coals
dense with old sunlight
your body dissolves
back into the dawn
your song
the silence breathing
all around you

Snowy Owl

You can stare at the sun
and not go blind
you ghost of a ghost
of a barn owl
ghost of snow
body of purest ash
marked by the fingers
of the charcoaled hands
that pulled you
still glowing from the kiln
you will never cool
mind full of mute
chrome yellow canaries
scratching
at the back of your eyes
beneath the black
of their pools
where silence is drowned
blinds the air

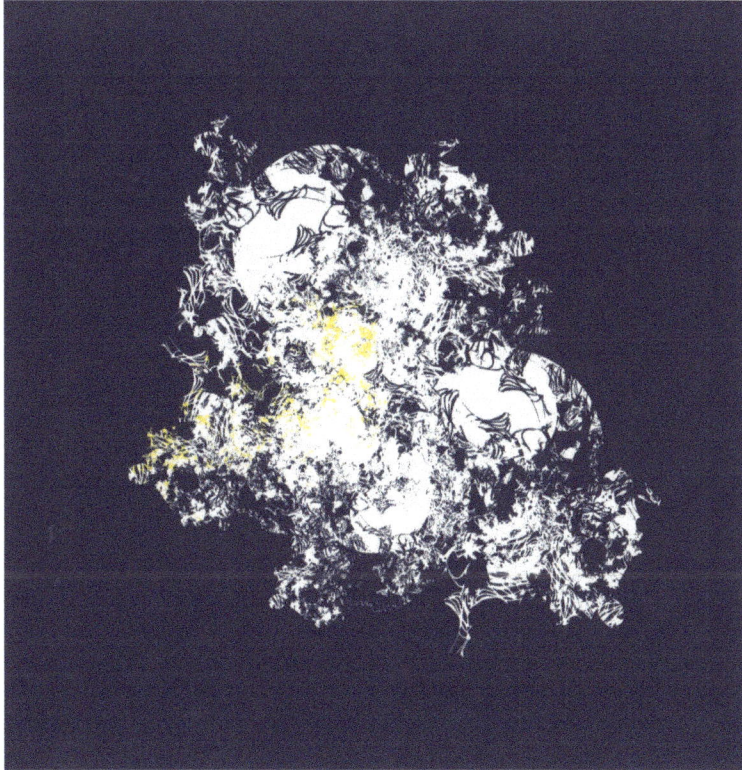

Firecrests

Flit between
the silver birches
tail-end of a firework
quietly setting
the world alight

Goldcrests

A brush stroke
of bumblebee yellow
blazes on the top
of their brains
a patch of forest fire
that never spreads
that can't be extinguished

Goldfinches

Blown into our dark room
a panic of gold daggers
then the sun takes back its breath
the curtains fall still
drips to the floor
in the distance a gold
glissando of rain
as the window turns blue
as a bruise

Starling

Born in brightness
in the quiet
above storms
watched the clouds
silver-slate cats
spark as they drag
their cheeks
down the length
of each other
now you weave
between the wires
of an electric fence
the current stretches
to touch the tips
of your flight feathers
tastes your darkness
sees the lightning
that cracked you open
now turned to smoke
burrowed deep
in the slick black
of your body

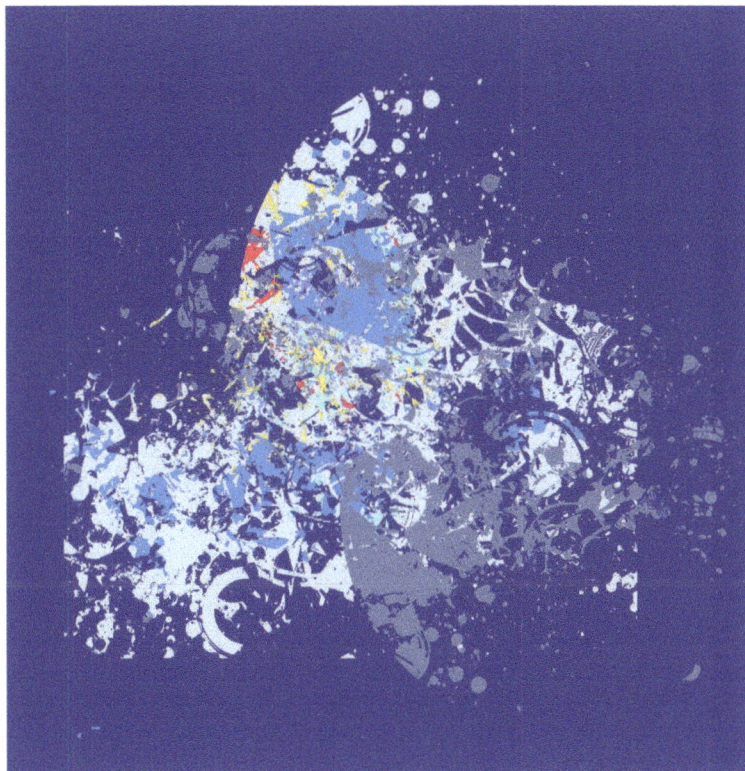

Shoals of Starlings

1.

Streaming through my wrists
my cupped hands full of flight
hold you close in my glittered arms
so you can feel the shimmer
as they change direction within me

2.

Slip sliding above the city
feathers like flints
striking the streetlamps
keeping the sun ticking over

3.

Slide beneath our feet
glide from puddle
to puddle
underneath the traffic

4.

Flew in the spray
of a comet's tail
their flint faces
covered in spittle

5.

Their broken black glass
settling before the forge
that will fuse them
turn them clear again

6.

As they sleep
stars scratch themselves
down their jet-black-breasts

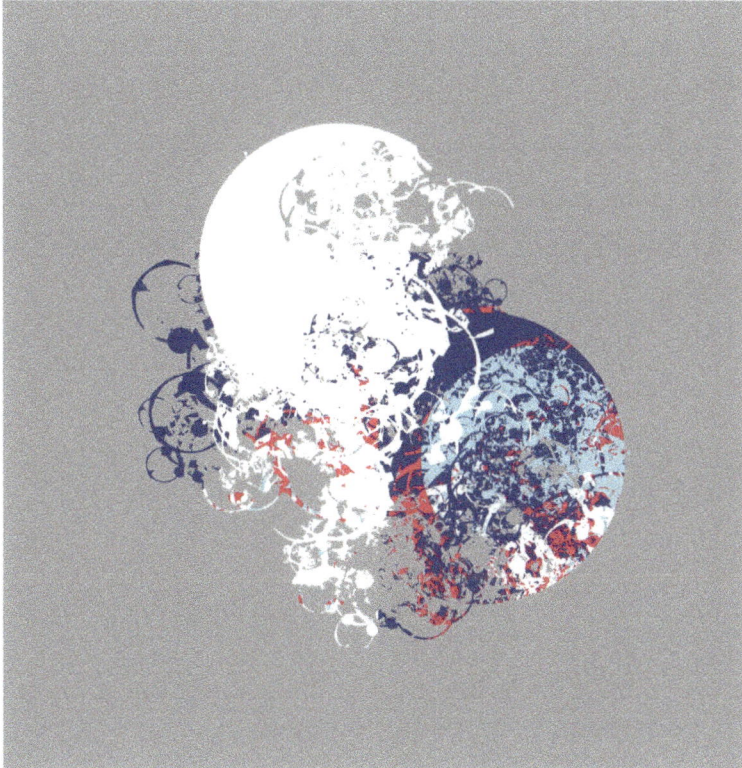

I'm not Starlings

A collective mind
full of maps and nebulas
following the currents of air
revealing the ghosts of rivers
that haunt the sky
the night a magnet
placed against my mind
furring the iron filings
of my thoughts
swivelling my poles
streaking a new star
through my headdress
placing a murmur
in my small
white-hot-heart

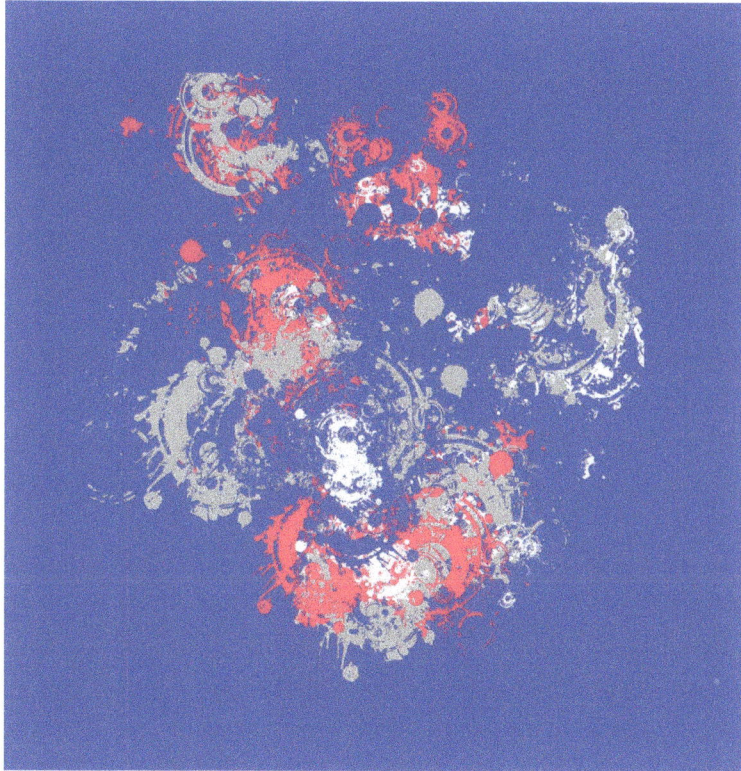

Herons

1.

Graceful umbrella
waiting to unlatch
from the riverbed
your spread slate
sparks in the rain

2.

Ballerina on stilts
pluck a fish from the river
supple as the silver you swallow
hunting an act of prayer

Little Egret

Sprout of lightning
rising from the mud
turning to chalk
touched by air

or are you
a spearhead of lightning?
lodged in the earth
refused to fade
along with the shaft

unlatched your legs
now spend your life
studying as you stroll
the dark that stilled you

Pheasants

1.

Chest-burster
of the hedgerows
beaten from bronze
carries the flames
to further fields

2.

Rusted tuba
night has a place to sleep
in the sewer of your mouth
coiling deeper into your
diminishing fallopian tubes
ovaries flood with stars
blood spreads around your
crushed body

broken wings in the wind
guttering like old fire
the rising sun
a held note
fading across the fields

Cormorant

Sooty gargoyle
wings ragged
as the flames
that stroked them
salt whispers
to the stars
held in your eyes
watching the tides
from the tip
of a rib
of a shipwreck
as the spindrift
with its faint kisses
slowly erodes
your face

Gannet

Scythe over skin
burnt wingtips
brush the sea
taunting it to rise
to taste the fire
further up the feathers
the waves scream
knifed in the dark

Robin

Heart a grenade
pin pulled at birth
inside of your breast
peppered in shrapnel

the snowman's conscious
all winter
spent whispering
to his disappearing heart

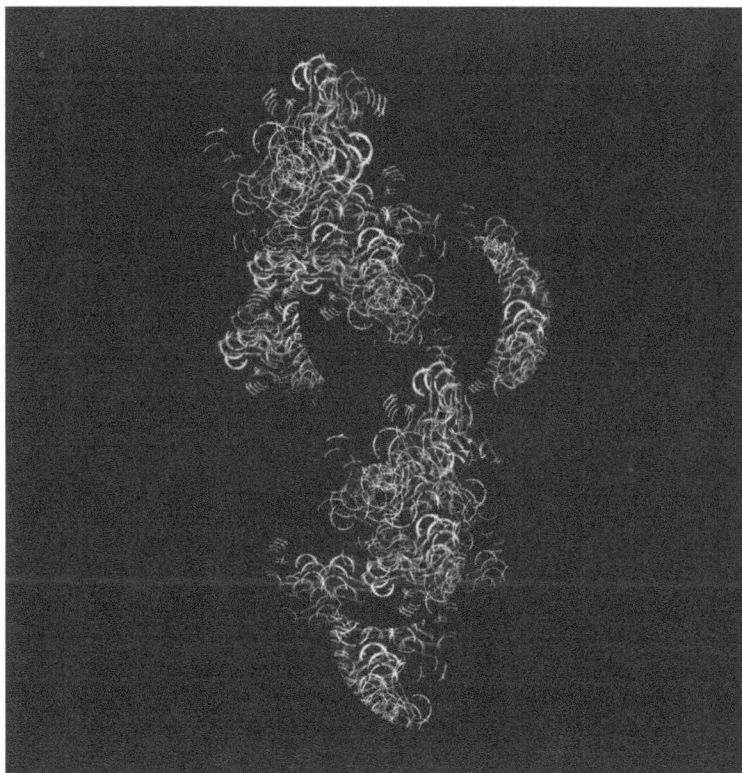

Wagtail

Timer set
tail ticking
made from discarded tin
off the watchmaker's floor

pinched like springs
inside your monochrome body
nobody ever sees
the colours freed

nobody witnesses
your tiny detonation
your mushroom sized
mushroom cloud
dispersing its spores

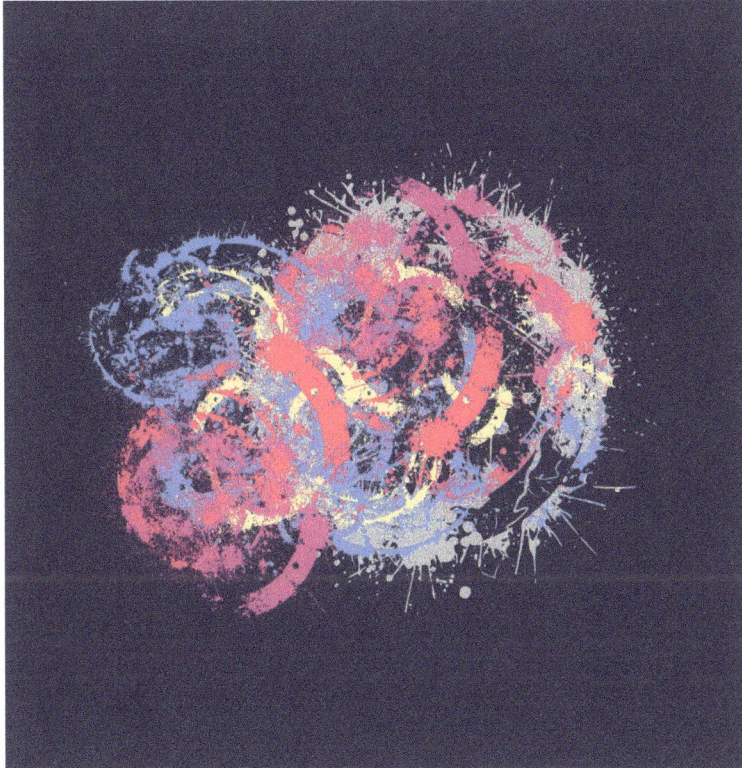

Blackcap

Compelled to consume
the white drops of mistletoe
makes you dream of the fire
that ravaged your brain
smoke damaged your mind

song bursts from you
a peal of bells
from a bombed-out church
hymn finished
you instantly forget
that you have sung

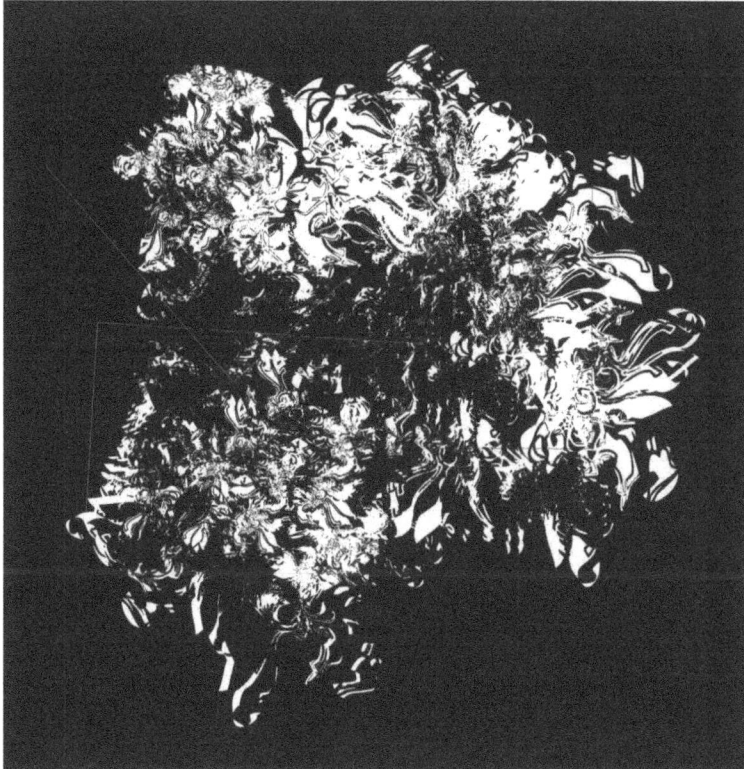

Sparrow

Shudders and squeezes
from the still smoking
hole in your chest

shivering on my tongue
its silence fills me
with your songs

Sparrows

Leaf litter kicked into life
flight not fire
feathers not flames
ash from the chorus

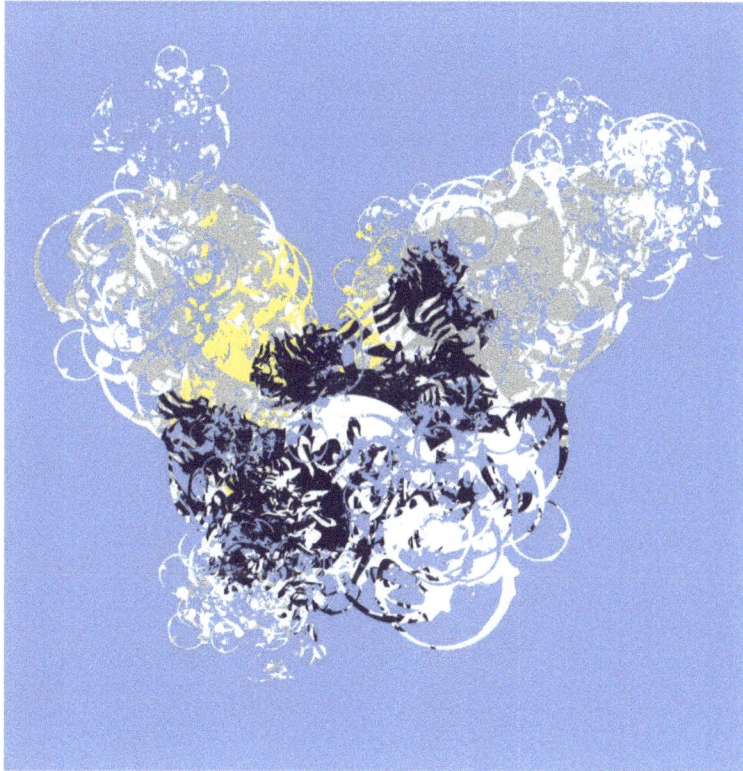

Skylarks

A chandelier
shivers in the sewer
in the belly of a whale
ghosts of skylarks
crowd its stems
their phantom songs
drip in the dark
tiny fields
sprout from the splashes
whisper
to the unseen
abandoned sky

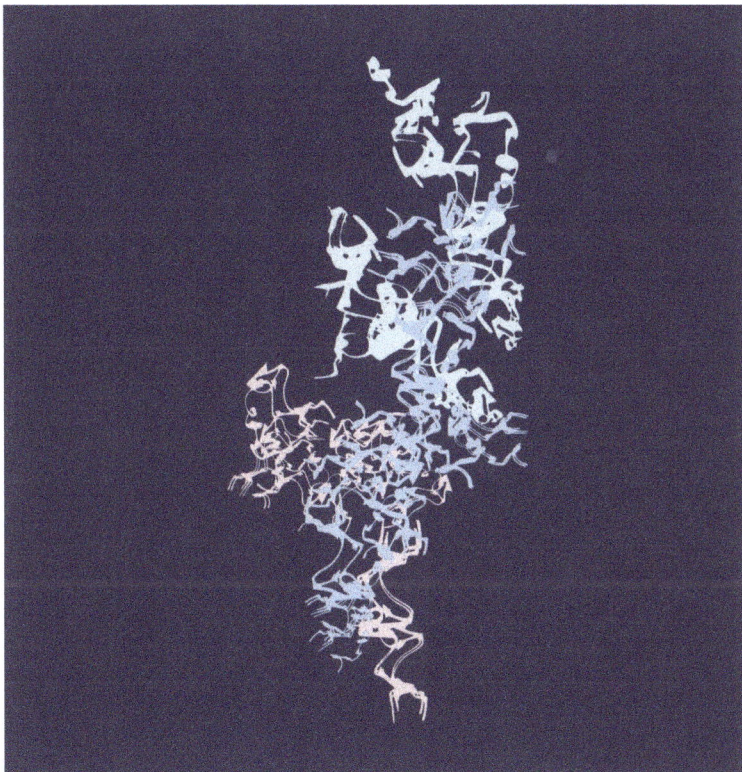

Skylark

Kissing the corners of sky
spilling songs upon our faces
sticky as cobwebs

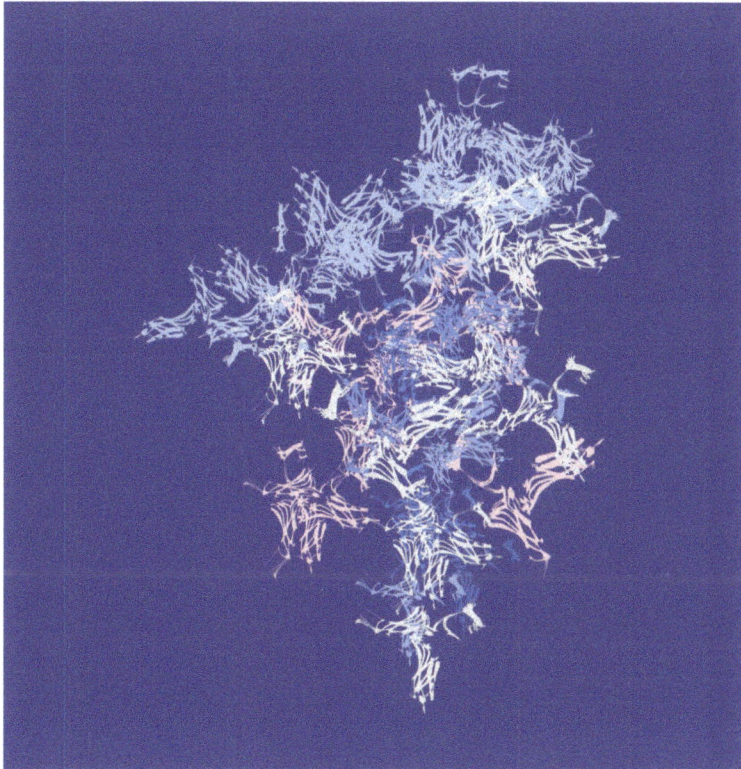

A Meeting

You shunned the night
shed your shawl of starlight
with breath of a barn upon you
in daylight came to meet me
briefly stunned by each other
before you fanned the pale fire
of your feathers
silent as silver took flight
darkening into pewter

one night it will be my turn to wait
knowing you'll come
and I'll stare
into your bottom-of-the-well-eyes
search for the moon
a small dropped white stone
bright as bone

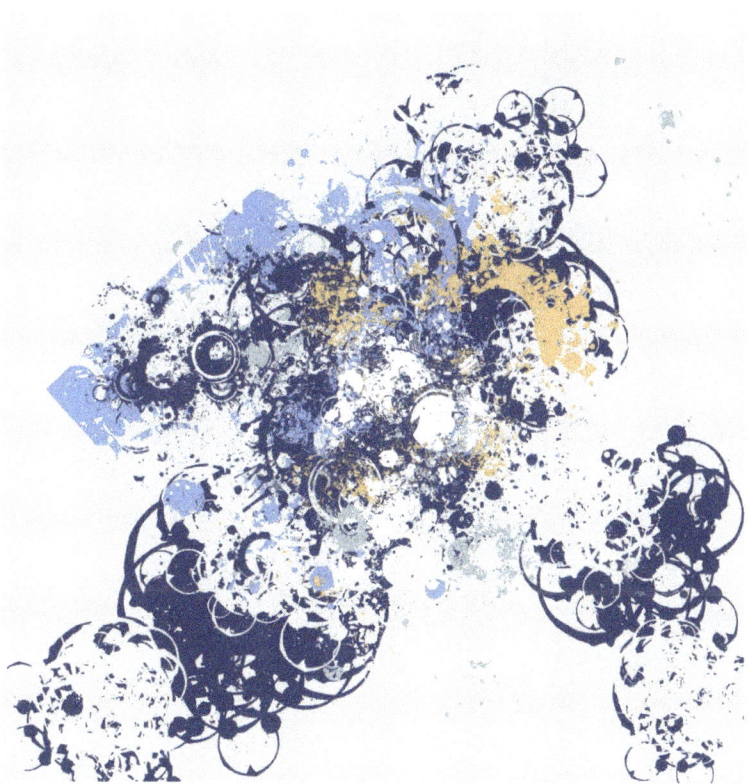

Kiss

Nuthatch creeps up my spine
starlings shatter in my mind
sparrows dust my shoulders
swallows bow my tendons
cormorant reveals its rags to the sun
peregrine slips into my chest
kingfisher re-surfaces
stained with rust from the riverbed
tawny owls tangle their calls together
hummingbirds sip at my weeping cuts
smoke of pink in the bruise of a pigeon's ruff
splinters of sky in the wings of a jay
a shower of firecrests sparks through my lungs
crowned with blue tits
crow hoods our faces
flame of a canary passed on our tongues
skylark spills its praise
magpie shreds its silver
barn owl skims the shadow stained fields
a wren buzzes in each chamber of my heart
swan unfurls from the dark

Murmuration

Is it the sashaying darkness that hypnotises?
sequined shadows
flare and fall before sleep

or is it the brightness of the blizzard they reveal?
lightning licking
the tip of every snowflake

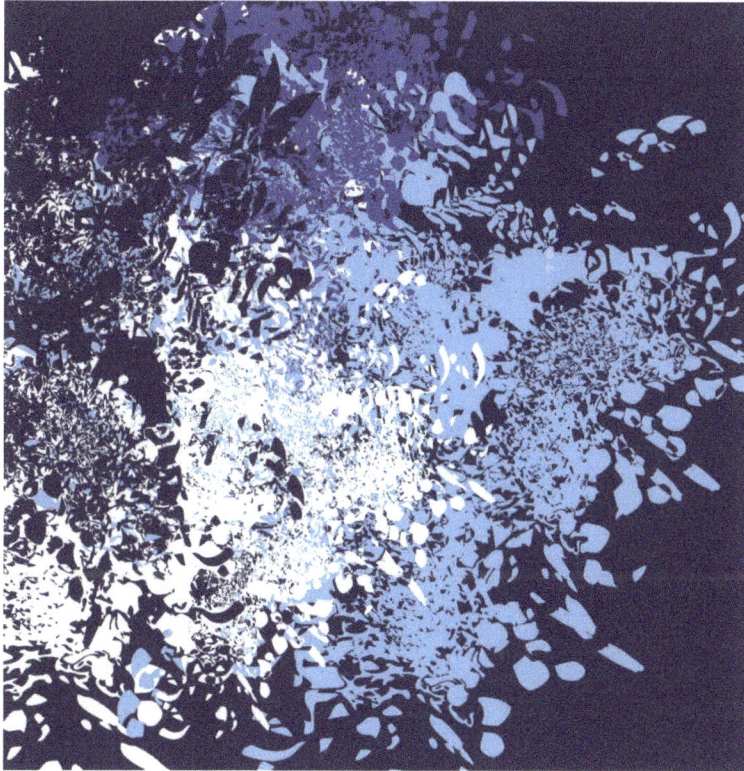

The hollowness of bird bones

Gives me hope
the way their marrow
is additional air
how their wings
extend their lungs

Hush

Sun a squatter
inside you

sea went quiet
held its breath

held my breath
holding you

the gloaming soughed and sighed
between our palms

your smile
chimed the dark

ships leaned
into each other's stillness

swayed like grass
swept by a barn owl

Playing invisible pianos in the dark

Is that all we're doing
playing invisible pianos in the dark
listening to the crumble of chords
leaves at the end of autumn
settling upon the desire paths
smoke tracing up through our fingers
whisper of sun and fields
rising for breath into our palms
hearing the starlings dream
from inside the pianos dark
hearing the next chord in the silence
before it's even played
even if it's never played

www.ingramcontent.com/pod-product-compliance
Lightning Source LLC
Chambersburg PA
CBHW061224270326

41927CB00025B/3486